Manufactured by Amazon.ca
Bolton, ON

13974900R00068